How Do You Kill

11 MILLION PEOPLE?

---•⊙⊙•---

WHY THE TRUTH MATTERS
MORE THAN YOU THINK

---•⊙⊙•---

ANDY ANDREWS

THOMAS NELSON
Since 1798

NASHVILLE   DALLAS   MEXICO CITY   RIO DE JANEIRO

Contact Andy
To book Andy for corporate events, call
(800) 726-ANDY (2639).
For more information, go to
www.AndyAndrews.com.

Published in Nashville, Tennessee, by Thomas Nelson. Thomas Nelson is a
registered trademark of Thomas Nelson, Inc.

Interior illustrations by Wayne Brezinka.

Thomas Nelson, Inc., titles may be purchased in bulk for educational,
business, fund-raising, or sales promotional use. For information, please e-mail
SpecialMarkets@ThomasNelson.com.

ISBN: 978-1-4041-8356-8 (IE)

Library of Congress Cataloging-in-Publication Data

Andrews, Andy.
  How do you kill 11 million people? : Why the truth matters more than you think
/ Andy Andrews.
      p. cm.
  Summary: "If the truth is what sets us free, what does it mean to live in a society
where truth is absent? How do truth and lies in the past shape our destiny today?
Through the lens of the Holocaust, Andy Andrews examines the critical need for
truth in our relationships, our communities, and out government"— Provided by
publisher.
  Includes bibliographical references.
  ISBN 978-0-8499-4835-0
1. Democracy—Philosophy. 2. Truth—Political aspects. 3. Truth—Social
aspects. 4. Political leadership—United States. I. Title. II. Title: How do you kill
eleven million people?
  JC423.A553 2012
  320.01—dc23   2011033402

Printed in the United States of America

12 13 14 15 QG 9 8

Author's Note

For many years I have been asked to speak to political gatherings of one type or another. And for many years I have consistently declined. Because the books I write are generally regarded as commonsense literature—novels that illustrate life's principles—I suppose many politicians have simply assumed that I was on their side. However, I am not an "us or them" kind of person. Actually, I am more of a "we" person.

Don't get me wrong—I do have some absolutes carved into my heart and mind, but I am optimistic enough to believe there is still common ground even with those of us who might disagree. Don't we all want the best for our country and a secure and prosperous future for our children? Of course we do. And I believe that we can talk about divisive subjects without screaming at each other.

Somehow, for the most part, our parents and grandparents managed to disagree with their neighbors and still remain neighborly. And they usually did it from their front porches. Today, most of us don't even have front porches. We have retreated to the backyard, where a single opinion can be isolated and enforced by a privacy fence.

Several years ago I asked myself these three questions: Where do we begin to find common ground in regard to what we want (or don't want) for the future of America? Is it possible to write something that doesn't use the words *Republican* or *Democrat*, *liberal* or *conservative*, yet conveys a message with which everyone could agree? Can it be written in a concise fashion allowing anyone to read it, clearly understand the message, and be empowered in less than fifteen minutes?

Here, then, is my answer to those questions.

—ANDY ANDREWS
ORANGE BEACH, ALABAMA

*The punishment which the wise suffer who
refuse to take part in the government, is to
live under the government of worse men.*[1]

—PLATO

For you shall know the truth, and the truth shall set you free."

'Those are probably the most famous words ever spoken on the subject of truth. Most of us accept that particular sentence at face value. It certainly resonates with our spirit. It just feels right. But what does it mean, really? And have you ever contemplated the meaning that comes to light by inverting this principle?

———

If it is correct that "you shall know the truth, and the truth shall set you free," then is it possible that if you *don't* know the truth, its absence can place you in bondage?

As a boy, I quickly learned that if someone found out the truth, I might get in trouble or I wouldn't get chosen or I wouldn't be as well liked. Yet my parents urged me to tell the truth and went so far as to promise I would not be spanked—if I only told the truth.

At Heard Elementary School, I told my fourth-grade classmates that Elvis Presley was my cousin. I suppose it was my way of courting popularity at the time. But Elvis was not my cousin. What I had publicly declared in the cafeteria was not true, and for a time, though it didn't seem possible, I became even less popular.

It was a good lesson and helped me determine that, in the future, I would tell the truth.

Once, when I was fifteen, a man in our neighborhood told me that he would pay me fifty dollars for a particular task of yard work. When I finished, he gave me twenty dollars and said that was the amount upon which we had agreed. It was the first time someone had ever looked me directly in the eye and purposefully told me something that was not true. I took note several years later when he was publicly shamed and financially penalized for another instance—entirely unrelated to me—of not telling the truth.

Through my formative years and on into young adulthood, the truth became a touchstone, a goalpost, something to strive for. The truth was always within my sight, usually respected but sometimes compromised.

Once, I watched on television as the president of the United States resigned his office in disgrace. At that time, it didn't occur to me that the nation was in so much turmoil—and the president was in so much trouble—not because of what had been done, but because he had lied about it.

AS AN ADULT, I have become a student of history. For some reason, I am fascinated by what people said and what nations did so many years ago. I am also interested in results—the outcomes these civilizations produced as they reacted to what people said and what nations did so many years ago.

I often wonder, do those outcomes have any bearing on us today? Should we be more careful students of the events and decisions that have shaped the lives and nations of those who have gone before us?

A long time ago I decided that if history were to be of any value in my life, I could not succumb to the temptation of convenience in regard to my personal beliefs or desires. In other words, I would not be able to categorize people and nations as "good guys" or "bad guys" to suit my political or religious beliefs. The truth in what I uncovered would have to trump everything I had ever been taught or believed. Quietly, I could only hope that what I had been taught and believed was true.

Sometime during my study of the Dark Ages and Middle Ages, I uncovered an odd paradox that exists in our minds about time gone by. It is a difference most people don't discern between history and the past. Simply stated, *the past* is what is real and true, while *history* is merely what someone recorded.

If you don't think there is a difference, experience an event in person and then read about it in the newspaper the next day, after witnesses have been interviewed. It might be shocking for many of us to realize that what we know as "history" can actually be a total fabrication, created from the imagination of someone with an ax to grind. Or perhaps, and it certainly happened in the Middle Ages, history was simply recorded by the man with the sharpest ax.

ON INTO WORLD conquest I read, now aware that to be assured of accurate information it would be vitally important that I confirm records and stories with transcripts and eyewitness accounts where possible.

The records surrounding the life of Joan of Arc—her triumphs, capture, fourteen-month trial, execution, retrial of nullification twenty years after her death, and subsequent canonization—particularly fascinated me. Hundreds of eyewitnesses testified over a period of almost thirty years as to what they personally saw or did not see.

Do we know the truth about the life and death of Joan of Arc today? One would hope so. She is the patron saint of soldiers, martyrs, prisoners, and the entire nation of France.

World history, for those who continue to study

it, becomes more defined during the seventeenth and eighteenth centuries, particularly during the American Revolution. Records by opposing forces and differing beliefs remain in relatively good shape and can still be examined by those wishing to do so.

The people of our present world retain a general awareness of historical time lines and a few specific dramatic events that shaped our lives. We occasionally read history or watch history presented on film. But in terms of why we do what we do, how we govern each other, what our society allows and why—very few of us intentionally connect the truth of the past with the realities of where we have ended up today.

So is the truth of the past even important? What about the truth itself? Beyond the elusive moral ideal by which most of us were raised—being honest and doing good—does the truth really, really matter?

To answer that question effectively, I would ask you another question . . .

How do you kill eleven million people?

OBVIOUSLY, MOST OF us have never even considered such a thing. Yet when I began to closely research our world's recent history—the last one hundred years—that particular question made its unsettling way into my mind.

How do you kill eleven million people?

Eleven million. The number is so large when the word *people* is attached to it that it becomes almost impossible to take seriously.

"Why eleven million?" you might ask. "What is the significance of that number?"

It is true: there is no *singular* significance in that number. And the actual number is 11,283,000—the number of people recorded who were killed by Adolf Hitler between the years 1933 and 1945.[2] Incidentally, that particular figure only represents institutionalized killing. It does *not* include the

5,200,000 German civilians and military war dead.[3] Neither does it include the 28,736,000 Europeans killed during World War II as a result of Hitler's aggressive governmental policies.[4]

Within the same parameters, we could have used the number of Cambodians put to death by their own government: slightly more than three million between the years 1975 and 1979. Three million—from a total population of eight million.[5]

We could have used the exact figure of 61,911,000. That is the number of people who were murdered by the government of the Soviet Union, shown by their own records, between the years 1917 and 1987. But only 54,767,000 of the men, women, and children put to death by the Communist Party were officially Soviet citizens. That is 14,322 human lives for every word in this book.[6]

During World War I, the highest leadership council of Turkey's Young Turk government decided to exterminate every Armenian in the country, whether a soldier already on the front lines fighting for the government or a pregnant woman. This government institutionally killed their own famous scholars, their own religious leaders, their own children, and ardent patriots of their own country. All two million of them.[7] We could have used that number instead.

In fact, during our world's last one hundred years, there are many different figures from which to choose. Three million in North Korea.[8] More than a million each in Mexico,[9] Pakistan,[10] and the Baltic States.[11] The choices available, and numbers of dead killed at the hands of their own governments, are staggering. And in other places around the world, they are just getting started.

But for our purpose, let's focus on the number that is probably the most well known to us—the eleven million human beings exterminated by the Nazi regime.

There are many lessons we have learned from that tragic period in history, but one particular part of the story remains quietly hidden from even the most brilliant of scholars. It is the answer to one simple question.

How do
you kill
eleven million
people?

ONLY A CLEAR understanding of the answer to this question and the awareness of an involved populace can prevent history from continuing to repeat itself as it already has, time and again.

To be absolutely clear, the *method* a government employs in order to do the actual killing is not in question. We already know the variety of tools used to accomplish mass murder.

Neither do we need to consider the mind-set of those deranged enough to conceive and carry out a slaughter of innocents. History has provided ample documentation of the damage done to societies by megalomaniacal psychopaths or sociopaths.

What we need to understand is how eleven million people allow themselves to be killed.

Obviously, that is an oversimplification, but think with me here . . . If a single terrorist begins to shoot automatic weapons in a movie theater containing three hundred people, the lone gunman couldn't possibly kill all three hundred. Why? Because when the shooting started, most of the crowd would run. Or hide. Or fight . . .

So why, for month after month and year after year, did millions of intelligent human beings—guarded by a relatively few Nazi soldiers—willingly load their families into tens of thousands of cattle cars to be transported by rail to one of the many death camps scattered across Europe? How can a condemned group of people headed for a gas chamber be compelled to act in a docile manner?

The answer is breathtakingly simple. And it is a method still being used by some elected leaders to achieve various goals today.

How do you kill eleven million people?

Lie to them.

ACCORDING TO TESTIMONY provided under oath by witnesses at the Nuremberg Trials (including specific declarations made in court on January 3, 1946, by former SS officers), the act of transporting the Jews to death camps posed a particular challenge for the man who had been named operational manager of the Nazi genocide. Adolf Eichmann, known as "The Master," was directed by written order in December 1941 to implement the Final Solution.

Eichmann went about the task as if he were the president of a multinational corporation. He set ambitious goals, recruited enthusiastic staff, and monitored the progress. He charted what worked and what didn't and changed policy accordingly. Eichmann measured achievement in quotas filled. Success was rewarded. Failure was punished.

An intricate web of lies, to be delivered in stages, was designed to ensure the cooperation of the condemned (but unknowing) Jews. First, as barbed-wire fences were erected, encircling entire neighborhoods, Eichmann or his representatives met with Jewish leaders to assure them that the physical restrictions being placed upon their community (in what later became known as ghettos) were only temporary necessities of war. As long as they cooperated, he told them, no harm would come to those inside the fence.

Second, bribes were taken from the Jews in the promise of better living conditions. The bribes convinced the Jews that the situation was indeed temporary and that no further harm would befall them. *After all*, they reasoned, *why would the Nazis accept bribes if they only intend to kill us and take*

———⊙⊙———

everything anyway? These first two stages of deception were conducted to prevent uprisings or even escape.

Finally, Eichmann would appear before a gathering of the entire ghetto. Accompanied by an entourage of no more than thirty local men and officers of his own—many unarmed—he addressed the crowd in a strong, clear voice. According to sworn statements, these were very likely his exact words:

Jews: At last, it can be reported to you that the Russians are advancing on our eastern front. I apologize for the hasty way we brought you into our protection. Unfortunately, there was little time to explain. You have nothing to worry about. We want only the best for you. You will leave here shortly and be sent to very fine places

———

indeed. You will work there, your wives will stay at home, and your children will go to school. You will have wonderful lives. We will all be terribly crowded on the trains, but the journey is short. Men? Please keep your families together and board the railcars in an orderly manner. Quickly now, my friends, we must hurry![12]

The Jewish husbands and fathers were relieved by the explanation and comforted by the fact that there weren't more armed soldiers. They helped their families into the railcars. The containers, designed to transport eight cows, were each packed with a minimum of one hundred human beings and quickly padlocked.

At that moment they were lost. The trains rarely stopped until well inside the gates of Auschwitz.

Or Belzec.

Or Sobibor.

Or Treblinka . . .

A list drawn up by the German Ministry in 1967 names more than 1,100 concentration camps and subcamps accessible by rail.[13] The Jewish Virtual Library says, "It is estimated that the Nazis established 15,000 camps in the occupied countries."[14]

And **that** is how you kill
eleven million people.

Lie to them.

But wait, you say.
This didn't happen overnight!
How did things get so
out of hand? How did it
get to this point?

THE NATIONAL SOCIALIST German Workers' Party, led by Adolf Hitler, rose to power during a time of economic uncertainty in a nation of people longing for better times. Germany was a modern, industrialized nation whose well-informed citizens enjoyed ready access to information by way of print and radio broadcast media.

Hitler was a man of the common people—not long before, he had been a lance corporal in the army—and his speeches were exciting and passionate. He promised more and better and new and different. He vowed rapid change and swift action.

According to record, what Hitler actually said in his speeches depended very much upon the audience. In agricultural areas, he pledged tax cuts for farmers and new laws to protect food prices. In working-class neighborhoods, he talked about redistribution of wealth and attacked the high profits generated by business owners. When he appeared before financiers or captains of industry, Hitler focused on his plans to destroy communism and reduce the power of the trade unions.

"How fortunate for leaders," Hitler said to his inner circle, "that men do not think. Make the lie big, make it simple, keep saying it, and eventually they will believe it."[15]

In *Mein Kampf*, Hitler's autobiography, he wrote, "The great masses of the people will more easily fall victim to a big lie than a small one."[16] The book was widely read by the German people at the time.

The masses believed him anyway.

Or at the very most, they ignored him. It is a fact that fewer than 10 percent of Germany's population of 79.7 million people actively worked or campaigned to bring about Hitler's change.[17] Even at the height of its power in 1945, the Nazi political party boasted only 8.5 million members.[18]

So the remaining 90 percent of Germans—teachers and doctors and ministers and farmers—did . . . what? Stood by? Watched?

Essentially, yes.

Mothers and fathers held their voices, covered their eyes, and closed their ears. The vast majority of an educated population accepted their salaries and avoided the uncomfortable truth that lingered over them like a serpent waiting to strike. And when the Nazis came for their children, it was too late.

YOU SEE, IT wasn't only the Jews who were persecuted. Today, most people are unaware that of the eleven million people exterminated, five million were not even Jewish. In Dachau, one of the largest and most infamous of all concentration camps, only a third of the population was Jewish.

We've all heard of the yellow triangles the Jews were forced to wear for identification. Do you know the other colors that were used?

Brown triangles identified gypsies and those of Roman descent. Purple triangles were worn by Jehovah's Witnesses, Catholic priests, and Christian leaders who ran afoul of the government.

Black triangles marked one as a vagrant—worn by any person lacking documentation when asked for proof of a permanent address. Blue triangles were forced on those who had moved to Germany from other countries, unless they were Jewish, in which case they wore yellow.

Red triangles were worn by a large and diverse group. You wore red if you were a member of a trade union, a Democrat, a Freemason, or any number of categories labeled as a "political non-conformist." Pink badges identified homosexuals, though any suspected perpetrator of a sexual offense such as rape or pedophilia was also given a pink triangle.

Green badges were given to common thieves and murderers. And since they were not suspect politically, these prisoners—called *kapos*—were often in charge of the others.

Purple badges. Red and pink and brown. Blue and black. All worn by mothers and fathers and children who were not the first to be selected for the camps. Their badges were worn—their fates altered—well after they got a good look at the yellow ones.

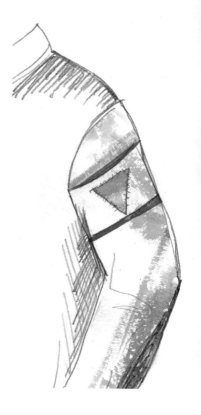

IN AT LEAST one German town the railroad tracks ran behind the church. An eyewitness stated:

> We heard stories of what was happening to the Jews, but we tried to distance ourselves from it, because we felt, what could anyone do to stop it?
>
> Each Sunday morning, we would hear the train whistle blowing in the distance, then the wheels coming over the tracks. We became disturbed when we heard cries coming from the train as it passed by. We realized that it was carrying Jews like cattle in the cars!
>
> Week after week the whistle would blow. We dreaded to hear the sounds of those wheels because we knew that we would hear the cries of the Jews en route to a death camp. Their screams tormented us.

We knew the time the train was coming and when we heard the whistle blow we began singing hymns. By the time the train came past our church, we were singing at the top of our voices. If we heard the screams, we sang more loudly and soon we heard them no more.

Years have passed and no one talks about it now, but I still hear that train whistle in my sleep.[19]

WITH ALL WE now know, does anyone believe that telling the truth will solve all a nation's problems? Of course not. But it *is* a beginning. In fact, speaking truth should be the *least* we require of our elected leaders! After all, what are *our* standards for being led?

You see, the danger to America is not a single politician with ill intent. Or even a group of them. The most dangerous thing any nation faces is a citizenry capable of trusting a liar to lead them.

In the long run, it is much easier to undo the policies of crooked leadership than to restore common sense and wisdom to a deceived population willing to elect such a leader in the first place. Any country can survive having chosen a fool as their leader. But history has shown time and again that a *nation of fools* is surely doomed.

INCREDIBLY, THERE ARE currently 545 human beings who are directly, legally, morally, and individually responsible for every problem America faces.

Have you ever wondered why America doesn't have a balanced budget? Have you ever in your life heard of a politician who wasn't *for* a balanced budget?

Have you ever heard a politician speak in favor of a complicated tax code that ordinary citizens would find difficult to understand? Then why do we have a complicated tax code that ordinary citizens find difficult to understand?

Meet the 545 men and women who enact every law, propose every budget, and set every policy enforced on the citizens of the United States of America: one president, nine Supreme Court justices, one hundred senators, and 435 members of the House of Representatives.

———◦◦———

By the way, have you ever noticed that if any one of us lies to them, it is a felony? But if any one of them lies to us, it is considered politics.

According to the United States Bureau of the Census, our population has now increased beyond 311 million people.[20]

To be clear, that's 545 of them and 311 million of us.

Can 311 million Americans ever hope to wrestle the power away from 545?

One would think so. But did you know that during the past quarter century, no presidential election has been won by more than ten million ballots cast? Yet every federal election during the same time period had at least one hundred million people of voting age who did not bother to vote!

KNOWING THAT THE quality of one's answers can only be determined by the quality of one's questions, let's ask some good ones . . .

Why do the ages of our world's greatest civilizations average around two hundred years?

Why do these civilizations all seem to follow the same identifiable sequence—from bondage to spiritual faith, from spiritual faith to courage, from courage to liberty, from liberty to abundance, from abundance to complacency, from complacency to apathy, from apathy to dependence, and finally from dependence back into bondage?[21]

Is lying to get elected acceptable? Even if the candidate's intention is to get elected in order to do good works?

Is there really any power in one's intentions anyway?

Have you ever noticed how we judge the "bad guys" by their actions and the "good guys" by their intentions?

Who are the good guys and who are the bad guys?

Would truth be a starting point for telling the difference?

What is our nation's course? Do you believe that one can determine a probable destination by examining the direction in which one is traveling? If so, where are we headed?

Can you hear the whistle and the wheels as the train comes down the track?

How
loudly are
you singing?

A Conversation with Andy Andrews

1. What are you trying to illustrate with this book?

Other than the subtitle, which is, "Why the truth matters more than you think," what this book illustrates is known as the Principle of the Path, which was first voiced by Andy Stanley. This principle states, "It is direction, not intention, that determines destination."[22] The Principle of the Path was also discussed in my book *The Final Summit*, a story about what happens when

---

historical figures like Winston Churchill, George Washington Carver, Joan of Arc, and others gather in order to solve a particular challenge. In *The Final Summit* the characters inadvertantly show that history itself is a path that can be examined at any point along the way in order to predict future results.[23]

Similarly, history is merely a broad version of our individual lives: Do we see a pattern in our good choices? Do these good choices lead to good results? Of course they do; therefore, let us continue to make choices just like those good ones that proved beneficial to our lives.

On the other hand, do we see a pattern in some bad choices we have made? Did those bad choices seem to connect the miserable dots that sank our life's results ever lower? Of course they did; therefore, let us determine that we will never make those choices again.

The only way we have to know a person who aspires to lead us is to listen to what he says and watch what he does. Frankly, what *I* might think of any current or past leader of the United States should be irrelevant to you. The questions most important in your life in regard to this subject should be: What criteria do you use to determine who leads your family? And what do *you* think?

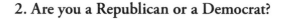

2. Are you a Republican or a Democrat?

As I stated in the author's note, I am not an "us or them" kind of person. I am a "we" kind of person. I am a concerned American citizen who demands integrity from those who seek to lead our country. Frankly, I believe candidates from both parties have lied to the American people. Furthermore, I believe that many are slipping dangerously close to creating a habit of lying and rationalizing that their purpose in doing so is "for our own good."

I don't want discussion of this book to devolve into partisan bickering. I did not write this book in order to compare Hitler or the Nazis to any of our current or previous leadership, Republican or Democrat. It might be interesting for the

reader to know that the phrase "redistribution of wealth" was not used in the body of this text in order to draw comparisons between Adolf Hitler and any specific person. Actually, I tried to find another way to phrase the point, but ultimately because it illustrated the Führer's style of saying what an audience wanted to hear—and because those particular words actually came from Hitler's mouth—I opted to go with what he really said.

It has become standard operating procedure for many politicians to say whatever is needed in order to get elected. This must stop. History's list is deep and wide and filled with the names of tragic governments whose citizens did *not* stop it.

—————⊙☉—————

3. Do you think the German population that allowed Hitler to lead them was a "nation of fools"?

Not necessarily. Germany, at that time, did not have the benefit of examining the history of the kind of tragedies of which they subsequently became a part. They were certainly a nation of misled people. They assumed that the leaders in whom they had placed their faith would put their best interests at the forefront. They were sincere in those beliefs. But as we know now, they were sincerely wrong.

4. Are the American people fools?

I think the jury is still out on that question. I have always considered the American people smart and industrious. Unfortunately, we have all known smart people who have done foolish things. As a group, when more than one hundred million of us don't bother to vote in a federal election, it certainly underscores the "apathy" portion of a nation's fatal sequence.

So are we too trusting? Probably. Are we downright gullible? I'm afraid evidence might support that assertion. But are we fools? I'll give it a "not yet."

5. Are you saying the United States will be the site of the world's next holocaust?

No, I'm not saying that it *will* happen. I am saying that it *could* happen. That's the whole point of the book. History shows that any people who are sheeplike in following their leadership (so long as their personal self-interests are satisfied) may one day awaken to find that their nation has changed in dramatic ways.

It doesn't take many people to lead a nation in a direction that has serious repercussions on the liberty of others. Indeed, most will agree that we have already given up liberties for various reasons, and we may never get them back. Under certain circumstances, things can take a very bad turn very rapidly. This cycle has repeated itself with many societies throughout history. Despite the solid foundation of our culture and political system, America is not immune. As philosopher George Santayana said, "Those who cannot remember the past are condemned to repeat it."[24]

We the people, however, can change this direction. But know this: our portion of history is being written today. What will be remembered about your contribution?

6. Who is lying to our country right now?

Sorry, but I'm simply not going to answer this question. The purpose of this book is to get *you* to answer that question for yourself!

My point is that each of us must stop blindly believing everything someone with an agenda says. Today, with the advent of the Internet's search engines and sites like YouTube, it is fairly simple to verify a politician's promises, voting record, personal life, and so on. So let's all work together. Post your proof online for all of us to read and pass along.

7. Why did you choose to write this book now?

Our nation is at a tipping point. Regardless of political views, people everywhere can sense it. Did you know that the United States of America is now the longest tenured government in the world? There are countries older than us, but as far as one continuous form of government, we are the oldest. Or the last, depending upon how you look at it.

If we don't demand honesty and integrity from America's leadership now—and reward that integrity with our votes—our leaders will lack the fortitude to make the hard decisions that must be made to change course.

If indeed our nation is in a state of crisis, then we need to change before it is too late to choose the direction of that change. We need the correct,

and best possible, people in office to make this happen. Some of them, of course, are already in office, but they need our help to surround them with men and women who will do what they believe is right and true.

I wrote this book for you to use as a tool. I wrote it for you to give away. I wrote it for you to discuss and preach about and read to your children. I believe that now, more than ever, America needs to be challenged and inspired to participate.

8. Obviously, there has been public debate and commentary from time to time about one situation or another, but have the American people ever been specifically cautioned about the long-term consequences of electing leaders who lack strong character?

Yes. Few remember the instance, but in retrospect, it is chilling to note the accuracy with which it was delivered. On the occasion of our nation's one hundredth birthday, in his centennial address to Congress in 1876, President James A. Garfield issued a warning widely reported in the press at that time. He said, "Now, more than ever before, the people are responsible for the character of their Congress. If that body be ignorant, reckless, and corrupt, it is because the people tolerate ignorance, recklessness, and corruption. If it be intelligent, brave, and pure, it is because the people demand these high qualities to represent them in the national legislature." Then, he added, "If [one hundred years from now] the next centennial does not find us a great nation . . . it will be because those who represent the enterprise, the culture, and the morality of the nation do not aid in controlling the political forces."[25]

9. How can we tell if a politician is telling the truth? Is there a way to know for sure?

You may remember the old joke: "How do you know if a politician is lying? If he's moving his lips." It's not that funny anymore, is it? Obviously, there is no certain way to know at the moment something is said. But remember this: past performance serves to reveal future behavior. A person who has exhibited a pattern of lying is a liar. I know that sounds rough, but can you think of another way to put it? This is why character in our leadership is so important.

In my book *The Final Summit*, Abraham Lincoln says to Joan of Arc, "Does adversity build character? . . . It does not. Almost all people can stand adversity of one sort or another. If you want to test a person's character, give him power."

Continuing, Lincoln says, "Now, since we are concerning ourselves here with the very future of humanity, let me add one thing more. Power corrupts. Trust me on this. And because power corrupts, humanity's need for those in power to be of high character increases as the importance of the position of leadership increases.

"We are discussing character, correct? Not intelligence. Some of the most intelligent leaders in history have brought disaster to their nations because intelligence is powerless to modify character. Great leadership is a product of great character. And this is why character matters."[26]

10. Who should we be listening to?

We should listen to ourselves, listen to common sense, and be mindful of—then heed—what we already know to be true. And we desperately need to be honest with ourselves! We must recognize that, as voters, we sometimes accept a lie when it suits our own self-interest. That's why polls sometimes show that Americans are in favor of throwing everyone out of Congress except *their* representative (at least among those knowing who their representative is).

Obviously, I cannot be in favor of cutting spending and entitlements *except* the ones that benefit me, or my district, or the place where I work. Unfortunately, that's often why we accept lies from politicians. It has become an accepted

political strategy for politicians to tell voters the lics we *want* to hear. We, in turn, reward them with elected positions even when we know we're not being told the truth.

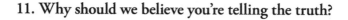

11. Why should we believe you're telling the truth?

The Internet can be a wonderful thing. I encourage readers to fact-check what I say in my book against multiple credible sources. That's why I included a bibliography. Read the books yourself . . . examine the record . . . it's all there for anyone to see. And might I add, that's exactly what we should do each time some politician or member of the media says something that doesn't ring true. If we really care to check things out, the lies aren't hard to detect.

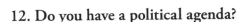

12. Do you have a political agenda?

Of course. And I sure hope you have one too. Here's mine: I want America's present and future leadership to embrace and live up to America's core principles as written by our Founding Fathers and set forth in our Constitution. In addition, I want the public to vigilantly hold them accountable for doing so. That is my political agenda.

13. Can you provide an example of a situation in our country that disingenuous leadership is enabling right now?

Certainly. There are many, but one such example was touched on briefly in the body of this work when I wrote, "Have you ever heard a politician speak in favor of a complicated tax code that ordinary citizens would find difficult to understand? Then why do we have a complicated tax code that ordinary citizens find difficult to understand?"

Look, I'm not the smartest guy in the world, but neither am I incredibly stupid. I believe that most folks like me find the days and weeks leading up to April 15 to be—how should I put this?—stressful. Not because we object to paying taxes, but because we fear doing it incorrectly and having to deal with the IRS if we have done so!

The US tax code is so convoluted and bewildering that few of us completely understand it. Yet many politicians actually derive power from it. Through the years, congressional representatives and senators have manipulated the tax code for myriad reasons, such as accepting donations or helping powerful members of their districts back home. In any case, a complex tax code provides a certain cover for shady wheeling and dealing at election time; therefore, there is not much incentive for politicians to simplify the process.

14. Who would you elect president?

Abraham Lincoln, but he won't run again. Beyond that, I am searching for that one special leader who can look us in the eye while telling us the painful truth in such a way that still manages to resonate with voters. That's a tough order, I know, but it can be done. Especially if smart people will get involved in the election process and actually vote.

Reader's Guide

1. We've all been faced with situations where we can choose to tell the truth or we can choose to lie. How have those lies affected your life negatively? In what ways can telling the truth make your life easier?

2. Do you think not telling the truth has a greater effect on you or on the other person?

3. Think about a time when you knew you were

---

being lied to. How did this make you feel? Did this have any effect on your feelings toward the other person? Explain your answer.

4. Is there a specific lie you've told in the past that has had a major impact on your life? What actions can you take to avoid lying in the future?

5. Some people like to measure their lies by how big or small they are. For instance, a white lie is considered to be a small lie that is supposedly harmless, or even beneficial, in the long term. Do you think it's ever okay to tell a lie? Explain your answer.

6. All lies have an impact on your life, your relationships, and the rest of the world. Do you

think the size of a lie determines how much of an impact it will have? Why or why not?

7. Should lying be acceptable when it is intended to protect someone else? Why or why not?

8. Why do you think it's easier to lie than to tell the truth in certain situations? Make a list of some situations you've been in where lying was an easier option than telling the truth. Explain why it was easier.

9. Think of the first lie you can remember telling. What do you think motivated you to not tell the truth?

10. Do you think learning about "the events

and decisions that have shaped the lives and nations of those who have gone before us" affects the way you interact with the world?

11. Sometime during Andy's study of the Dark Ages and Middle Ages, he uncovered an odd paradox: *the past* is what is real and true, while *history* is merely what someone recorded. Explain what this means to you.

12. Andy states, "Very few of us intentionally connect the truth of the past with the realities of where we have ended up today." How important is the truth, and what effect does it have on our future? Why do you think we have a difficult time connecting the truth of the past with the realities of where we have ended up today?

13. Why do you think the eleven million people sent to Nazi concentration camps believed Hitler and were willing to go? Do you think people's level of power has an effect on how easy they are to believe?

14. Hitler said, "Make the lie big, make it simple, keep saying it, and eventually they will believe it." Why is a simple and big lie easier to believe than one that is small and detailed?

15. Andy asks a big question: "Does anyone believe that telling the truth will solve all a nation's problems?" What do you believe?

16. How do you answer this question: "Is lying to get elected acceptable? Even if the candidate's

intention is to get elected in order to do good works?"

17. What does it mean to "judge the 'bad guys' by their actions and the 'good guys' by their intentions"? Which matters more: your actions or your intentions?

Resources

After reading this book, you may be interested in taking steps toward becoming more involved in your country's direction. The Internet is a wonderful tool for accomplishing this. You can find out how to do any number of things such as contacting your congressional representative, registering to vote, learning more about your state's and city's elected officials, learning when your city council meets, and more, all by doing a simple Internet search.

I also encourage you to seek wisdom at your local library and bookstore. Add others' knowledge and experience to your own. Of course, you need to be diligent in this pursuit and make sure your sources are reputable. You cannot believe everything you hear. Take time, compare, and consider what you are hearing and reading.

Most importantly, never stop looking for the truth. As long as we have our sights set on the truth, we are moving in the right direction.

Notes

1. Plato, quoted in Ralph Waldo Emerson, "Eloquence," *Society and Solitude* (Boston: James R. Osgood & Co., 1870), 56.
2. Rudolph J. Rummel, *Democide: Nazi Genocide and Mass Murder* (New Brunswick, NJ: Transaction, 1992), 85–86.
3. Ibid.
4. Ibid., 14.
5. Rudolph J. Rummel, *Statistics of Democide* (New Brunswick, NJ: Transaction, 1992), 48.
6. Rudolph J. Rummel, *Lethal Politics: Soviet Genocide and Mass Murder Since 1917* (Piscataway, NJ: Transaction Publishers, 1990), 16.
7. Rummel, *Statistics of Democide*, 78.
8. Ibid., 178.
9. Ibid., 187.
10. Ibid., 153.
11. Ibid., 164–77.
12. Neal Bascomb, *Hunting Eichmann* (New York: Houghton Mifflin Harcourt, 2009), 6.
13. www.enotes.com/topic/List_of_Nazi_Concentration_camps.
14. Jewish Virtual Library, http://www.jewishvirtuallibrary.org/jsource/Holocaust/cclist.html.

15. http://brainyquote.com/quotes/authors/a/adolf_hitler_2.html.

16. Adolf Hitler, *Mein Kampf*, trans. James Murphy (New York: Mariner, 1998).

17. www.mongabay.com/history/germany/germany-historical_background_population.html.

18. http://wn.com/nsdap?orderby=published.

19. Erwin W. Lutzer, *When a Nation Forgets God* (Chicago: Moody, 2010), 22.

20. US Census Bureau, US & World Population Clocks, http://www.census.gov/main/www/popclock.html.

21. Andy Andrews, *The Heart Mender* (Nashville: Thomas Nelson, 2010), 141–42.

22. Andy Stanley, *The Principle of the Path: How to Get from Where You Are to Where You Want to Be* (Nashville: Thomas Nelson, 2009), 14.

23. Andy Andrews, *The Final Summit* (Nashville: Thomas Nelson, 2011).

24. George Santayana, *The Life of Reason, or: The Phases of Human Progress*, vol. 1 (New York: Charles Scribner's Sons, 1905), 284.

25. James Garfield, "A Century of Congress," *Atlantic*, July 1877, 63, 64.

26. Andrews, *The Final Summit*, 176.

Bibliography

Andrews, Andy. *The Final Summit*. Nashville: Thomas Nelson, 2011.

Bascomb, Neal. *Hunting Eichmann*. New York: Houghton Mifflin Harcourt, 2009.

Hitler, Adolf. *Mein Kampf* (James Murphy Translation). New York: Mariner, 1998.

Lutzer, Erwin W. *When a Nation Forgets God*. Chicago: Moody, 2010.

Reese, Charley. "The Five Hundred and Forty Five People Responsible for America's Woes." www. informationclearinghouse.info.

Rummel, Rudolph J. *Lethal Politics: Soviet Genocide and Mass Murder Since 1917*. Piscataway, NJ: Transaction Publishers, 1990.

Stanley, Andy. *The Principle of the Path: How to Get from Where You Are to Where You Want to Be.* Nashville: Thomas Nelson, 2009.

www.census.gov

www.historyplace.com

www.jewishvirtuallibrary.org

www.nuremberg.law.harvard.edu

www.Spartacus.schoolnet.co.uk

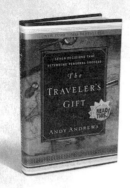

The
TRAVELER'S GIFT

New York Times Bestseller

SEVEN DECISIONS THAT
DETERMINE PERSONAL SUCCESS

ISBN: 978-0-7852-6428-6

An extraordinary experience awaits David Ponder. He finds himself traveling back in time, meeting leaders and heroes at crucial moments in their lives—from Abraham Lincoln to Anne Frank. By the time his journey is over, he has received seven secrets for success—and a second chance. *The Traveler's Gift* offers a modern-day parable of one man's choices—and the decisions that make the difference between failure and success.

The FINAL
SUMMIT

"A roadmap for all of humanity
to follow and cherish."

ISBN: 978-0-7852-3120-2

In the spirit of its *New York Times* bestselling predecessor, *The Traveler's Gift, The Final Summit* explores the historically proven principles that have guided our greatest leaders for centuries. Andrews combines a riveting narrative with astounding history in order to show us the one thing we must do...when we don't know what to do.

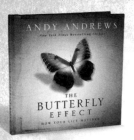

THE
BUTTERFLY
EFFECT

HOW YOUR LIFE MATTERS

ISBN: 978-1-4041-8780-1

"Every single thing you do matters. You have been created as one
of a kind. You have been created in order to make a difference.
You have within you the power to change the world."

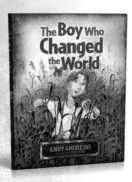

The **Boy** Who
Changed the **World**

Everything You Do Matters

ISBN: 978-1-4003-1605-2

The Boy Who Changed the World reveals the incredible truth that everything

YOU do matters—what you did yesterday, what you do today, and what you

will do tomorrow. Every choice you make, good or bad, can make a difference.

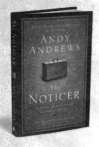

THE NOTICER

New York Times Bestseller

Based on a remarkable true story, *The Noticer* beautifully blends fiction, allegory, and inspiration. It provides simple, yet powerful distinctions about love, relationships, value, and integrity and will inspire readers to take that first step toward a major life change.

ISBN: 978-0-7852-2921-6

THE HEART MENDER

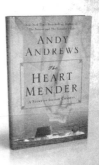

In *The Heart Mender,* a small town must prepare itself for the worst the world has to offer, and Josef and Helen must reconcile their pasts to create a future. Andy Andrews once again provides a unique blend of historical fact and engaging fiction showing the power of forgiveness.   ISBN: 978-0-7852-3103-5

THE LOST CHOICE

From the author of the *New York Times* bestseller *The Traveler's Gift* comes a gripping quest to uncover mankind's destiny. Elegantly blending gripping fiction, extensive research, and a powerful message of hope, *The Lost Choice* illuminates the timeless principles for transforming your life and the world.   ISBN: 978-0-7852-6139-1

RETURN TO SAWYERTON SPRINGS

This is a story that reflects upon the seemingly ordinary parts of our everyday lives—and how they are actually extraordinary parts of something much greater. Savor the time you spend in Sawyerton Springs. You might just find another hometown you want to claim as your own!   ISBN: 978-0-9819709-1-2

CONTACT ANDY

To interact with Andy through Facebook and Twitter, visit
ANDYANDREWS.COM

Teachers, don't forget to download your free companion curriculums at
ANDYANDREWS.COM/EDUCATION

To book Andy for a speaking engagement, call
(800) 726-ANDY (2639)